The Trabue Woods
Book of Values

blue ocean press

tokyo

The Trabue Woods
Book of Values

Martha R. Bireda

blue ocean press

tokyo

Most blue ocean press publications are available at special quantity discounts for bulk purchases for sales promotions, premiums, and educational needs.
Please contact us for more details.

Published by:

blue ocean press, an Imprint of Aoishima Research Institute (ARI)
#807-36 Lions Plaza Ebisu
3-25-3 Higashi, Shibuya-ku
Tokyo, Japan 150-0011

mail@aoishima-research.com
URL: http://www.aoishima-research.com

ISBN: 978-4-902837-20-X

THE TRABUE WOODS

BOOK OF VALUES

The traditional values held by the pioneers that settled the Trabue Woods community enabled the community to survive and to thrive. These values passed generation to generation, from 1885 to the late 1960's, were learned by the author herself as a girl growing up in the Trabue Woods community. Using old photographs and newspaper articles, the eight core values learned by the children of Trabue Woods are shared with young readers ages 9-13. The values taught in Trabue Woods are typical of those held by the descendants of slaves who established communities after the turn of the century. This book, originally written for the youth of Trabue Woods, has much to teach youth everywhere about values and character.

DEDICATION

This book is dedicated to Bernice Andrews Russell, social activist, humanitarian, African American historian, and the inspiration for the Blanchard House Museum of African American History and Culture of Charlotte County, Florida.

Bernice Andrews Russell

BERNICE ANDREWS RUSSELL

Bernice Andrews Russell was a proud woman. She was proud of her ancestry, her heritage, and her community. This pride inspired her to want to preserve the memories that shaped her life. Her greatest desire was that the children of Trabue Woods would "know who they were" so that they too could share her sense of pride.

WHY WE SHOULD LEARN ABOUT VALUES

Values are what a group of people feel are important. Our values help us to decide what is right or wrong. They guide our actions. They are like signs on the highway, they point out the right direction in which we are to go. Our values help to determine our character. When we say that a person has good character, we are talking about their values.

This book is about values. One way in which we can learn about values is to study history and learn about the values of historical figures. In this book, we will learn about the values of a group of African American pioneers who settled in southwest Florida in 1885, and helped to establish the town of Trabue, later called Punta Gorda, on the Charlotte Harbor. While these African Americans lived in many parts of what became known as Charlotte County, they established their own special community named Trabue Woods.

Just 20 years after the end of slavery, these African Americans built a thriving community. They were men and women of good character. Their values helped them to be successful in establishing the Trabue Woods community and in being an important part of the settlement of Punta Gorda and Charlotte County. These African American pioneers were guided by eight values.

What do you think these values were?

In this book, we will read about the values learned by the children who grew up in the Trabue Woods community and how these values were passed on to four generations.

NEW WORDS

Some words that you read in this book will be new to you. When you come across a word that you do not know, look it up in the dictionary. Our language is always changing and has changed much since the 1900's. Some words and phases that you will read in the old newspaper articles will not be familiar to you, in fact, you may find them to be funny. One word that you will see used in the old newspaper articles is "colored". This word was used to describe black people or African Americans during the early 1900's. When you come across "old" words or phases, ask an elder to help you to understand their meaning.

AFRICAN AMERICAN LIFE IN THE LATE 18th AND EARLY 19th CENTURIES

The values of the African American pioneers who settled in Trabue Woods came from two sources. There were both the values of their ancestors who came from Africa and the values adopted by African Americans to help them cope with the hard times they experienced as slaves and as freedmen.

The African American pioneers were either born enslaved themselves or the children of parents who were slaves. These pioneers, like other African Americans were very hopeful that they would enjoy the same rights and freedoms as other Americans after the end of the Civil War and slavery. For over ten years after the slaves were freed and during Reconstruction, schools were established for the ex-slaves and African American politicians were elected to office.

In fact, two of the African American pioneers living in Punta Gorda had been politicians during Reconstruction. Owen B. Armstrong, a teacher and carpenter, had been delegate to the 1868 Constitutional Convention in Florida, and served as a Leon County (Florida) commissioner from 1869 - 1870. He was also one of the four African American men to participate in Punta Gorda's first election. He was an active Republican until 1904.

Robert Meacham, a minister who had helped establish AME churches in Florida, was the postmaster of Punta Gorda from 1889 - 1891. He was forced to resign in 1892. Mr. Meacham had been one of the most important Reconstruction leaders in Florida. He was a delegate to the 1868 Constitutional Convention and served in the Florida Senate from Jefferson County for ten years.

During the Reconstruction period, 1865 – 1876, the laws provided protection for the Freedmen, but when Reconstruction ended in 1877, life again became very difficult for African

Americans. African American politicians were forced out of office, African Americans lost the right to vote, lost their jobs, and faced extreme violence directed towards them. Many of the pioneers who settled in Trabue Woods, came from northern Florida and from other southern states such as Georgia, South Carolina, and Alabama where life for African Americans was especially hard. They came to what was still considered to be the "frontier" of southwest Florida to escape the prejudice and violence they faced elsewhere.

THE VALUES OF TRABUE WOODS

- Spirituality

- Family

- Children

- Education

- Work

- Self-reliance

- Community

- Equality

THE VALUE OF SPIRITUALITY

BELIEF: God will provide.

A thatched palmetto hut like this one was the site of the

first worship service held in Punta Gorda.

Faith in God was one of the most strongly held values of the pioneers who settled in the Trabue Woods community of Punta Gorda. They believed that God would "make a way for them out of no way" and help them to survive however hard the times were that they faced.

Dan Smith, a member of the survey team that came to *Trabue* in 1885, organized the first religious service. After the train tracks for the Florida Southern Railway were completed and the first train arrived, Smith held the church service under a thatched palmetto hut. The first congregation was made up of blacks and whites of all denominations.

The establishment of Bethel African Methodist Episcopal Church was the result of this first religious service. After Dan Smith married Louisa Evans, a Baptist, he along with Caine Dorsey founded St. Mark Progressive Baptist Church. The value of spirituality was so important, that by 1916, there were four churches in the Trabue Woods community.

Sunday was a very special day in Trabue Woods and much of the day was devoted to serving God. Most people attended Sunday School and Morning Service, went home to have Sunday Dinner by 2:00 P.M., then came back for Evening Service by 6:00 P.M.

They also attended a weekly prayer meeting and Bible study. The church not only served the spiritual needs of the people but the social needs as well. The church provided for the needy in all ways.

THE PUNTA GORDA HERALD

April 24, 1913

Punta Gorda colored people are to have another church building. The members of the M.E. Church North are to build. E. Green of the board of trustees has placed an order for the materials and the contract has been let to M.J. Martin.

November 27, 1915

A big revival meeting lasting several weeks was concluded Sunday night at the A.M.E. church (colored), and as a result Pastor H.W. Gray says thirty-three new members have been added to the roll of the church and two to the Baptist church. Of those joining, the A.M.E. church, twenty-eight are to be baptized Sunday; fifteen to be immersed and thirteen sprinkled. The immersion will take place at an early-hour of the forenoon in the Bay just north of the boat sheds.

WHAT DID I LEARN?

1. Why do you think the value of "faith in God" was so important to the people of Trabue Woods?

2. How did the people of Trabue Woods demonstrate their strong faith in God?

3. What does " God will provide" mean to you?

4. Is the value of "faith in God" important to you? Why? or Why not?

LIVING HISTORY ASSIGNMENT

1. Interview an elder; ask them to tell you about the first churches that were established in Trabue Woods.

    If you do not live in Charlotte County, you may ask an elder about the first houses of worship established in your community.

2. Write a paper telling how the churches of the early 1900's are the same as and different from churches today.

THE VALUE OF FAMILY

BELIEF: When one has, all have.

Three generations.

Mrs. Cornelius Ponder, with her daughter and granddaughter.

Next to God, the family was the greatest source of strength for the early settlers. The Trabue Woods community was made up of strong families that worked together to provide a better life for all.

The pioneers that settled in Trabue Woods understood the value of family. During slavery, many African American families were torn apart. Children were sold away from parents, and parents from children. After slavery ended, husbands and wives searched for each other, and parents went to find their children. The experiences of slavery made family ties very important to African Americans.

To the people of Trabue Woods, family did not only mean a mother, father, and children. Family meant grandparents, aunts, uncles, cousins and even people who were not blood kin. In Trabue Woods, people considered "godparents" and "play" brothers and sisters to also be a part of the family.

Family members depended upon each other. They lived together, worked together, shared food, and money. Families also played together. The whole family had picnics, went to baseball games and "excursions" together. As soon as they were able, the men who settled in Trabue Woods sent for their parents, sisters, and brothers to join them. As family members "got on their feet", they in turn sent for another relative. During the 1940's when many of the young people who grew up in Trabue Woods went up north in search of better jobs, they stayed with relatives who had gone before them. Like their ancestors had done many years before, "when they got on their feet", they sent for younger brothers and sisters to join them in the North.

Older brothers and sisters also worked so that younger ones could finish high school and go off to college. As each brother or sister graduated from college, they were expected to help the next one. In some ways, the college education of one belonged to the whole family.

Saving money to buy land and build a house of their own was a major goal of most of the families that lived in Trabue Woods. By 1900, only 15 years after the first African Americans arrived in Punta Gorda, 37% already owned their own homes.

By working together, the families were also able to establish businesses. One of the most successful families in business was headed by Mack and Illinois Gollman. For many years, the Gollman family owned businesses that served the community and provided jobs for residents.

Gollman Family Home

The Punta Gorda Herald

June 7, 1895

A special train will leave Punta Gorda at 6 o'clock next Thursday morning, June 13, for Tampa and Picnic Island. The fare will be $1 for adults and 50 cents for children. Two front coaches will be especially for colored passengers. Cooling refreshments will be served aboard the cars. The train will arrive in Tampa at 11:00 A.M.

March 14, 1918

Ben Coleman, well known colored man, has the lumber on the ground to build a $1200.00 cottage in the neighborhood of the colored public school.

WHAT DID I LEARN?

1. What does "when one has, all have" mean to you?

2. What did the word "family" mean to the pioneers?

3. Why was being a part of a strong family so important to the pioneers?

4. Why was buying land and owning a home important to the residents of Trabue Woods?

5. On the cover of this book is a photograph of Willie and Annie Mae Haynes, and their children. Mr. and Mrs. Haynes believed that "if our children can look up to us, they will never look down on themselves". Why do you think that they believed this? How do you think this belief affected their children and who they grew up to be?

LIVING HISTORY ASSIGNMENT

1. Interview a member of one of the pioneer families that still lives in Punta Gorda; or interview one of the elders in your community. Ask them to tell you about their family.

2. Draw a family tree for one of the pioneer families, or for the family of one of the elders of your community.

3. Talk to an elder in your family; ask them to help you to draw a family tree for your family. Ask them when your family first came to the community where you now live. Ask him or her to tell you about the early experiences of your family.

THE VALUE OF CHILDREN

Belief: Children are our future.

Annual Spring Festival

Baker Academy - 1950's

Children were very special in the Trabue Woods community. All of the adults wanted to provide a better life for the children than the one they had known growing up.

In Trabue Woods, all adults were responsible for teaching and guiding children. The children understood that they must respect and obey all adults in the community.

Much of what was taught and expected of children living in Trabue Woods was known as "home training". Home training had to do mostly with learning respect and proper manners.

The most important rules of home training were:

1. Respect yourself.
2. Respect your family.
3. Respect the elderly.

A family's name was very important and children were taught and expected not to do anything to bring shame to themselves or to the family. Respect for the elders was most important. In the African tradition, ancestors are very highly respected and elders and since elders are considered to be closest to the ancestors, they are very special. To talk back to, roll one's eyes at, or suck one's teeth in the presence of an elder could get a child into big trouble.

Children could not listen to or interrupt the conversations of elders. Most important, whenever a child saw an elder they were to speak to them.

Good manners were expected of children at all times. There were always women in the Trabue Woods community who took responsibility for teaching etiquette and manners to the children.

During the 1950's and 1960's, "Miss Edna" (Mrs. Edna Thomas) hosted teas and dinner parties so that children in Trabue Woods could learn the "social graces".

In the community, through church and school, the children of Trabue Woods learned pride in their race and heritage. In both church and school, the children learned the African oral tradition.

31

At church, children had to take part in religious programs and pageants. Every child in the community, from the oldest to the youngest had to memorize and recite a Christmas and Easter speech.

In school students also learned to "stand and deliver" as part of the oral tradition. The school gave monthly recitals in the community in which all grades took part and a program at the end of each school year to celebrate the closing of school and to honor the graduates.

"Giving back" was a value learned by all of the children who grew up in Trabue Woods. They knew that, like their parents and other adults in the community that, when they grew up, they too would have to contribute to the community by "serving" in some way.

Children followed in their parent's footsteps. Archie

Bailey, Annie Mae Haynes, and Martha Andrews started the NAACP in 1930. The next generation, Berlin Bailey, Booker T. Haynes, Sr., and Bernice Andrews Russell, all took an active role in the civil rights movement and community affairs.

Dinner party hosted by "Miss Edna".

1950's

THE PUNTA GORDA HERALD

May 8, 1913

Tuesday night, the boys of the 4th and 5th grades will present a mock trial, the famous watermelon case. Wednesday night, the girls will render a very beautiful cantata, "A Dream of Fairyland". These exercises will take place at Miller's Hall. A small admission charge to cover expenses.

B.J. Baker, Principal

COLORED SCHOOL TO CLOSE

The closing exercises of the colored public school will begin Sunday, May 12, at St. Marks Progressive Baptist Church at 2:30 p.m. A short program will be rendered by the grades consisting of songs and readings. There will be two graduates, Olivia A. White and Carrie L. Smith. The Baccalaureate sermon will be delivered by Rev. M.L. Cherry. Wednesday and Thursday nights, 15th and 16th insts., concerts will be rendered at the Masonic Temple. All are cordially invited to the exercises.

_____ *B.J. Baker Principal*

May 20, 1915

Colored School To Close

The closing of the colored public school will begin Sunday, May 23rd. This feature of the exercises will be conducted at St. Mark Progressive Baptist Church, consisting of a short program rendered by the pupils of the 5th, 6th and 7th grades, followed by the annual sermon by Rev. Maj. L. Cherry. Exercises will begin at 2:30 p.m.

Song___Holy, Holy.
Responsive Reading.
Reading of the Scripture___Rev. M. L. Cherry
Invocation____Rev. H.W. Gary.
Song___Never say fail.
Paper___"What are we living for," Edith Dwight
Recitation___The lost chord, Olivia White.
Paper____Time to Cultivate honor. J.C. Coleman
Vesper Song____School.
Paper___"Is this a Christian nation?"by Frank Andrews.
Duet___Summer Blossoms, Edith Dwight, Olivia White
Annual Sermon___Rev. M.L. Cherry

All invited, seats free.

The annual concert will be given at Miller's Hall, Wednesday

and Thursday nights, May 26 and 27.____B.J. Baker, Principal

WHAT DID I LEARN?

1. What is "home training"?

2. What was expected of children growing up in Trabue Woods? What do you think of those expectations?

3. Why was it important for the children of Trabue Woods to be involved in plays and programs? In what ways are you learning to "stand and deliver"?

4. What does the school closing program in the newspaper tell you about the values of the students who attended the colored school?

5. What does it mean to "give back"?

6. How would your life be different if you had grown up in Trabue Woods during the early 1900's?

LIVING HISTORY ASSIGNMENT

1. Interview an elder; talk to him or her about how bringing up children has changed from the "old days" to now.

2. Interview Mr. Lindsey Williams, the Punta Gorda Historian, or another historian in your community, and find out what games children played during the early 1900's; write a paper.

Mrs. Cornelius Ponder

MRS. CORNELIUS PONDER

(1870-1934)

Mrs. Ponder believed that being a midwife was a God-given talent and that helping to bring life into the world was one of the greatest gifts one could give.

Mrs. Ponder was one of the first midwives in Punta Gorda and is the only midwife listed in the 1900 census. Mrs. Ponder was very religious and depended upon God to help her to do her work.

For Mrs. Ponder, being a midwife was "a labor of love". Many times she was not paid, however she always gave the best of care to all of her patients.

Most of the children who grew up in Trabue Woods, and most in Punta Gorda, were delivered by Mrs. Ponder.

1.   What is " a labor of love"?

2.   What were the values of greatest importance to Mrs.

        Ponder?

THE VALUE OF EDUCATION

BELIEF: You have to get an education to be successful in life.

Students of old colored school.

Early 1900's

The pioneers of Trabue Woods placed a very high value on education. All of the parents wanted their children to have more education than them. They wanted their children to go as far as they could in school. Finishing high school was felt to be absolutely necessary and going on to college was very desirable. Each generation that grew up in Trabue Woods was more educated than the one before.

Knowledge and learning are values of the African culture that is the heritage of the pioneers of Trabue Woods. Before Africans were taken as slaves and brought to the New World, there had been great universities in Africa. The pioneers learned the value of education from the stories told by their parents and grandparents who had been enslaved. Although slaves were punished for learning to read and write, many took the risk and learned anyway.

The pioneers believed that "an education is the one thing that no one can take away from you". Even adults who had not learned to read and write were eager to do so. By 1900, just 35 years after the end of slavery and 15 years after Punta Gorda was settled, 70% of the residents of Trabue Woods could read and 60% could read and write.

Dan Smith, the community leader, did not learn to read and write until taught how to by his wife Louisa.

The first school for African Americans in Punta Gorda was a little private Adventist school. Mrs. Giles taught students on the porch of her home. Parents paid 15 cents per week to have her teach their children. "When the water came out of the Peace River, the men would piggy back their children to the porch".

In 1902, the citizens of Trabue Woods founded a public school for "colored" children. The collected money, bought land, and worked together to build the school. Dan Smith was sent to find a teacher. Benjamin Baker was the first teacher of the colored school. Having a school for colored children was so important that two adults, Dan Smith and Alex Stephens, attended school with children so that the community would have the quota of students needed for the County to pay for a teacher for the colored school.

Schools were segregated and the colored school did not receive as much money as the white school to operate. African American students often had no books or old books and less supplies than the white school. The colored school only went to the eighth grade. Parents made great sacrifices so that their children could finish high school. Some parents worked hard to pay tuition for their children to attend a private boarding school, while most lived away from home with relatives in towns where they could attend a colored high school. The residents of Trabue Woods believed that every child could learn; there were no excuses for failing to go as far in school as possible.

Not only learning to read and write, but being an outstanding student was very important. When students in Trabue Woods made the Honor Roll, their names were published in the Punta Gorda Herald weekly newspaper for all to see. To be on the Honor Roll brought great pride to the students, their parents, and the whole community.

THE PUNTA GORDA HERALD

November 3, 1922

Students who qualified for the honor roll at Baker Academy:

Lily Mae Reddish

Frances Roberts

Huldy Andrews

Albert Williams

Odessa Reddish

Bernice Andrews

Shellie Lee Slay

Catherine Andrews

Mayola Ponder

Emma Gagley

Lillian Gollman

Ida Mae Scott

December 19, 1902

Rev. L.A. Johnson and A.B. Coleman, two public spirited colored citizens have raised $50 with which they have bought four lots just north of the Colored Baptist Church, whereupon to build a school house.

August 20, 1908

The Negroes have a good public school with one teacher and about 35 students.

May 8, 1913

The Punta Gorda Colored School will close May 18th. The Graduating exercises will take place at the A.M.E. Church, May 18, 7:30 P.M. Baccalaureate service by Rev. M.L. Cherry, this city.

The public has been cordially invited. Seats free.

October 13, 1922

Baker's Academy, the local public school for colored pupils, with three teachers is making good progress. The enrollment is 95.

WHAT DID I LEARN?

1. Why was getting an education so important to the
    residents of Trabue Woods?

2. What hardships did African Americans face in getting
    educated? Why did they not get discouraged?

3. How did educating their children help the Trabue Woods
    community to become successful?

4. How was being a student in the early 1900's different
    from being a student now?

LIVING HISTORY ASSIGNMENT

1.   Talk to an elder who attended the Baker Academy or another African American school before Integration. Do a report on what school was like in the "old days". Ask about the subjects that students took, what teachers were like, and what was expected of students.

Professor Benjamin J. Baker

BENJAMIN JOSHUA BAKER

(1872-1942)

When Benjamin Baker was born, slavery had only been abolished for eight years. Despite the risk of punishment, his parents had learned to read. They promised each other that their son, Benjamin, would learn to read, write, count, and speak correctly.

Benjamin Baker did not go to school until he was ten years old, and then only for two or three months each semester because he had to work in the fields. By the time he was 19, however, he passed the test to become a teacher.

In 1902, Benjamin Baker was hired to teacher at the Colored School in Punta Gorda. He was a very religious man who had high moral principles. Even though he was a very strict teacher and principal, he was loved by all of His students who called him "Fess".

1. What values guided Benjamin Baker?

THE VALUE OF WORK

BELIEF: A colored man has to work twice as hard to succeed.

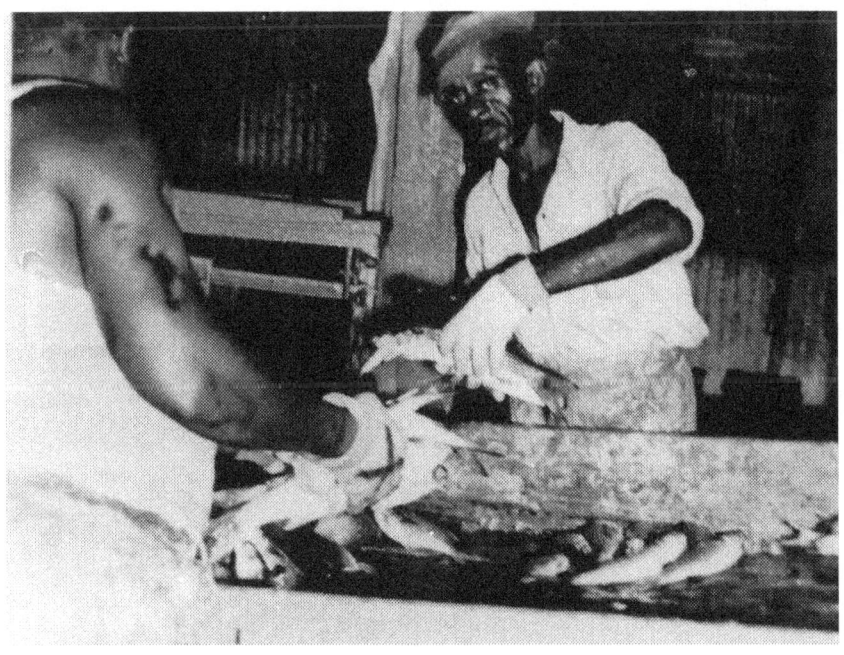

Andrew "Mullet" Owens

One of the best workers at the Punta Gorda Fish Company.

The men and women who settled in Trabue Woods worked hard to build a better life for themselves and their children. They did all of the kinds of work that were necessary in Punta Gorda. Many men worked as day laborers that helped to lay the brick streets and build the "big hotel". Some worked in the phosphate mills and turpentine stills. Others were skilled workers such as carpenters, draymen, machinists, and shipwrights. Often the women were employed as washerwomen and cooks.

Most men were employed in the fishing industry. In the early days, commercial and "sports" fishing was the major industry in Punta Gorda. The African American fishermen fished in small boats called "sharpies". They fished everyday from before sunrise to after twilight, what they called "dark to dark". They would spend up to five days out fishing; they would ice their fish and bring them back to the fish house for packing. African Americans worked on the docks packing the fish to be transported by train or truck to many other states.

The African Americans who settled in Trabue Woods were not only interested in working hard but achieving as well. They worked twice as hard as other workers and took great pride in their work. Many times the African American workers would be described as the "fastest" or "best" at the work that they did.

THE PUNTA GORDA HERALD

September 16, 1915

Peter W. Miller, a popular colored citizen, after doing very satisfactory work for the government for nine months at Sparrow's Point, Md., came home last week and was warmly greeted by his many friends.

January 30, 1919

That well known colored citizen, Chas L. Pratt, has decided to return to his old profession of tarpon guide. He has had years of successful experience in the work, for which he is getting his boat and other equipment ready.

January 29, 1904

The sharpie "D.C. Smith" named for her owner and builder who is an industrious colored man, has proved to be one of the best boats of the fishing fleet. She is navigated by her owner and is bringing in lots of fish.

September 19, 1904

The yacht "Ethel Q." has just come off the ways of Cleveland where she underwent an overhaul. She is now in "apple pie order" for business. Her skipper is Capt. Green, the well known colored seaman.

WHAT DID I LEARN?

1. We often see the words "expert", "best", and "industrious" used to describe the pioneers. What does this tell you about the values and character of these men and women?

2. Why did the pioneers believe that they had to work twice as hard as others (whites) to succeed? Why did they not get discouraged?

LIVING HISTORY ASSIGNMENT

1. Interview an elder who can tell you about the fishing industry in early Punta Gorda. Ask him or her about Mr. Andrew "Mullet" Owens, Mr. Gaitor, the fastest oyster opener, Mr. Ollie Washington, and Mr. Bud Whitehead, two of the best tarpon guides. If you do not live in Punta Gorda, you can interview an elder and ask them to tell you stories about the interesting personalities in the community that they remember from their youth.

2. Write a report on "Sharpie Town", where the African American fishermen lived. Interview Mr. Lindsey Williams, the historian to get your information. If you do not live in Punta Gorda, write a report about early African American owned businesses in your community.

THE VALUE OF SELF-RELIANCE

BELIEF: We must do for ourselves.

The Cleveland Marine Steamways -

Owned by George Brown

The settlers of Trabue Woods not only worked hard at their jobs, but even harder to establish businesses of their own. They believed in not just finding a job but in creating jobs for themselves and other people in the community. In 1902, African Americans owned a hotel (the Ingram Hotel), a rooming house (Miss Carrie Washington), a barbershop (The Star Shaving Parlor, A.B. Coleman) and a grocery store (O.B. Armstrong). By 1927, 20 African American owned businesses were listed in the Punta Gorda City Directory. They built businesses to meet the needs of the people living in Trabue Woods. There were grocery stores, restaurants, dry cleaners, rooming houses, a barbershop, a drugstore, and even a venetian blind factory. Some businesses were smaller and run by one person. There was someone in the Trabue Woods community from which residents could buy ice and wood.

The pioneers also established lodges and organizations to help residents when they became ill or when a family member died. Some of the dues that members paid to their lodges were used to pay the cost of their funeral when they died; these were called "burial societies". In the Trabue Woods community, most people belonged to one or more of these lodges and organizations: the Masons, the Oddfellows, the Herods of Jericho, the Eastern Stars, the Lily Whites, and the American Woodmen. All of these organizations were also known as "self-help" organizations.

THE PUNTA GORDA HERALD

February 6, 1913

The framework for the new hall for the colored Oddfellows of this city has been erected and the building will be rushed to completion as soon as further materials are received. It occupies a portion in the Eastern edge of the town and is being built under the supervision of contractor M.J. Martin.

April 18, 1918

The ladies of the Colored Peoples Auxiliary of the Punta Gorda Red Cross are busy trying to get the boys of Punta Gorda ready for camp. Our membership is twelve and we would be glad if other friends would join us.

A. Ambrose, Sec.

May 9, 1918

Mrs. Charles Pratt went to Jacksonville as a delegate to the annual meeting of the grand lodge of the Household of Ruth I.O.O.F. jurisdiction of colored people.

January 15, 1904

STAR SHAVING PARLOR

A.B. Coleman, Proprietor

HAIR CUTTING, SHAVING,

SHAMPOOING AND TREATING

OF ALL FORMS OF SCALP DISEASES

First Class Work. Satisfaction Guaranteed.

CHARCOAL FOR SALE.

February 6, 1908

E. Ward, colored, wishes it known that he has a fine new surrey, with a fast, gentle horse, for taking people anywhere in- or about town.

September 10, 1908

George Brown, the popular colored stevedore and expert 1908 machinist, is putting in up-to-date steam ways at Cleveland, of which he will take personal charge. This means he has given up his job at Port Inglis and will remain at Cleveland.

WHAT DID I LEARN?

1. Why was it so important for African Americans to own their own businesses during the early 1900's?

2. Why were the lodges and organizations called "self-help" societies?

LIVING HISTORY ASSIGNMENT

1. Read the 1927 Punta Gorda Business Directory.

    Write a report the types of businesses that African Americans owned. What businesses owned by African Americans were not located in Trabue Woods? If you do not live in Charlotte County find a business directory in your community that lists the businesses owned by African Americans in the 1920's.

2. Interview an elder and then write a report about the early lodges and organizations established by the pioneers in Trabue Woods. You may also report a report about the early lodges and organizations established by the elders in your community.

George Brown at age 75, holding

a neighbor's son, John Howell Teter, Jr.

GEORGE BROWN

(1868-1951)

George Brown, a carpenter, came from Charleston, South Carolina to Cleveland, Florida in 1891. He brought a crew of other African Americans with him to build drying bins and barges for the DeSoto Phosphate Mining Company. In 1897, George Brown started his own shipyard, called Cleveland Marine Steam Ways. Mr. Brown's steam way, the first and largest in Southwest Florida operated until the 1930's. Mr. Brown was a major landowner in Punta Gorda. He was a good employer and is considered to be the first "equal opportunity" employer in Florida. Mr. Brown was a very generous man who helped many people.

1.   What is an "equal opportunity" employer?

2.   What values made Mr. Brown a good businessman?

THE VALUE OF COMMUNITY

BELIEF: The whole is greater than the parts.

Five of the seven Bailey brothers

whom all served in WWII.

The Trabue Woods community was like one big family. Each person, even children, had to do their part to make the community work. Families in Trabue Woods shared the vegetables grown in gardens as well as oranges, grapefruits, mangoes and guavas from trees. The fishermen shared their catches. The men helped each other build houses, the women made quilts together, and those with cars transported those without.

The community not only worked together but played together as well. On Saturday nights, there were plays, concerts, and boxing matches at Miller's Hall. Churches sponsored picnics and hay rides. On Saturday and Sunday afternoons, the whole community turned out to watch the local team play baseball. There were also outings by boat to the nearby islands.

The pioneers were not only concerned about Trabue Woods, but the whole community of Punta Gorda as well. From the time that the first seven African American men arrived, they were active in civic affairs in Punta Gorda. Four African American men signed the papers to incorporate the city of Punta Gorda in 1887. The pioneers volunteered their time and money to help to build the new city.

THE PUNTA GORDA HERALD

May 25, 1894

The Florida Southern brought down quite a large excursion of colored people last Monday from Bartow and other points to the north. The principal attraction while here was a baseball game between the "Ninos" of Bartow and Punta Gorda.

December 26, 1902

Our colored people had a big Christmas. They began on Tuesday with an entertainment by the Dixie Comedy Company in the Colored Masonic Hall and followed up with private social affairs every night since.

June 15, 1916

Punta Gorda colored citizens entertained a large number of the colored citizens of Ft. Myers who came up on the special excursion Monday. In a baseball game in the afternoon

Punta Gorda girls beat the Ft. Myers girls and the Ft. Myers men were the winners over the Punta Gorda men.

September 24, 1908

The colored citizens of Punta Gorda held a meeting at their Masonic Hall and agreed to help build the wharf. Those contributing included: S.P. Andrews, Lem Jackson, D.C. Smith, John Smith, C.L. Pratt, P.W. Miller, John Davis, E. Ward, T.W. Sanders, Charles Smith, Howard Lewis, Louis Zanders, Sam Kenady, Geo. Brown, J.J. Mitchell, A.B. Coleman, Frank Sanders, John McGee.

October 1, 1908

A large force went down the bay for piling Monday morning and so Punta Gorda's public dock has started: the following colored citizens went: Lem Jackson, E. Ward, H. Lewis, L. Zanders, C.H. Smith, Ben Andrews.

October 30, 1919

The Colored People Civic Association last week donated

$8.00 to the fund to build a fountain to the new artesian well at

the intersection of Marion Avenue and Taylor Street.

Patriotism and loyalty to the country were also values that were held by the pioneers. During WWI the community showed their patriotism by buying" Liberty Bonds". Young men volunteered to fight in WWI and WWII. The patriotism of one family in particular from Trabue Woods was outstanding. All five of the famous Bailey Brothers served in WWII. There was at least one brother in each of the four branches of the Armed Services.

THE PUNTA GORDA HERALD

October 17, 1918

Our colored people are proving their patriotism in more ways than one. They have contributed liberally to the Red Cross and to Belgian relief; some of their best men are in the army and others not fit for military service are working in ammunition factories "up north"; many of them are buying Liberty Bonds and now comes St. Mark's Progressive Baptist church, of which Rev. M. L. Cherry is pastor, and puts an advertisement in this paper calling upon every body to buy Liberty Bonds. As long as we have such people as these, there is no doubt we will beat the Huns, "horse, foot, dragoon," Kaiser and all.

WHAT DID I LEARN?

1. Why was it necessary for the Trabue Woods community to be a "family"?

2. How were the pioneers from Trabue Woods involved in the civic affairs of Punta Gorda?

3. What does this sentence from the newspaper article mean? "As long was we have such people as these, there is no doubt we will beat the Huns, "horse, foot, dragoon," Kaiser and all".

LIVING HISTORY ASSIGNMENT

1. Interview an elder who grew up in Trabue Woods.

    Ask him or her to tell you about all of the good times

    they had "down the street". You may also interview elder

    in your community and ask him or her about all of the

    good times they had in your old African American

    business district.

2. Interview an elder; ask him or her to tell you about the

    "war years". What was life like for African Americans in

    the United States at that time?

Daniel C. Smith

DANIEL C. SMITH

(1865-1935)

"When Dan Smith, the local colored man, came here in 1885, there were only 15 people here of who 8 were white and 7 black. He and Sam Kenady, also colored are the only ones of the original 15 who are left."

"Dan" Smith was one the five African American survey team that Gov. Albert Gilchrist brought to Trabue in 1885. He was a deeply religious man who organized the first religious meeting in Punta Gorda in 1886. He was a fisherman by trade but became a businessman who bought property and sold oranges from his grove. Dan Smith was sent to find a teacher for the Colored School. He convinced Benjamin Baker to move to Punta Gorda. Dan Smith and Alex Stephens enrolled in the school to make up the required number of pupils needed for the

County to hire a teacher. Dan Smith was a very respected leader both in the Trabue Woods community and the city of Punta Gorda.

1.   What values helped to make Dan Smith a

respected leader?

THE VALUE OF EQUALITY

BELIEF: We are Americans too.

Archie Bailey, Annie Mae Haynes, and

Martha Andrews organized the first NAACP

in Punta Gorda in 1933.

When the first black and white men arrived to build the railroad and establish the town of Punta Gorda, they worked side by side. African Americans owned businesses "downtown" that served white customers and many African Americans and whites lived close together. Between 1887 and 1891 life for African Americans all over the United States began to change, even in Punta Gorda as "Jim Crow" laws were passed. Jim Crow laws were state and local laws that required racial segregation or the separation of black and white people in all public places. These laws meant that African Americans could not go freely like whites into schools, restaurants, hospitals, or other public places. Signs that read "Whites Only" or "Colored" were placed over water fountains, waiting rooms, and restrooms.

In Florida, from 1885, African Americans could not go to school with whites or marry whites. From 1905, African Americans had to ride in separate railroad cards and sit in separate waiting rooms. They also could not use the public libraries, swimming pools, or beaches.

When the Plessy vs. Ferguson Supreme Court decision was passed, African Americans became "second-class" citizens. The schools were segregated and the "colored" school received much less money to support it than the white school. In 1915, the "colored citizens" of Punta Gorda held a mass meeting to protest inequalities in the funding of the colored school for "colored" citizens.

THE PUNTA GORDA HERALD

MASS MEETING OF COLORED CITIZENS

Whose Souls Breathe the Refreshing

Zephyrs of True Democracy Take Action

Punta Gorda, Fla.,

April 15th, 1919

We the colored citizens of Punta Gorda, Fla., at a mass meeting held at the A.M.E. church, to discuss the failure of the County School Board of DeSoto County to carry out its contract of seven (7) months with the teachers of our Public School, owing to the shortage of funds adopted the following resolutions.

Whereas the time has come for all races to throw off the yoke of bondage, and to have self determination, and to enjoy the blessings of the coming World's Democracy, for which we have so liberally contributed, and whereas no nation, race or people can enjoy or demand the rights accorded to them by the provisions of their government, without an education and

Whereas we are called upon to all our places as loyal American citizens, in the defense of the rights of the United States, pass the same examination, keep down Bolshevism, (which can only be done by educating), and

Whereas we responded so liberally to the call of the government, through the buying of War Saving Stamps, Liberty Bonds, supporting the Red Cross Work to the last ditch, picking up the United War Workers Campaign with as much eagerness and force, and all of these were only to us as a starter and bracer for the VICTORY LOAN, which faces us and also mean to put that OVER TOP, among us.

We feel that we have not had a square deal, and our efforts to win Democracy for the world have failed in bringing that to the Colored American Citizens of this community will proceed to maintain our public school by raising through public subscription, one hundred ($100) dollars, the amount necessary, (having half of said amount in hand already) to carry out the unexpired term of the Punta Gorda Public School.

In 1930 three citizens from the Trabue Woods community, Archie Bailey, Martha Andrews, and Annie Mae Haynes organized the first chapter of the NAACP to fight for the equal rights of colored citizens in Punta Gorda and Charlotte County.

WHAT DID YOU LEARN?

1. What was "Jim Crow"? How were the African American pioneers treated during Jim Crow?

2. What was the "Plessy vs. Ferguson" decision? How did it affect African Americans?

3. What feelings and beliefs were expressed by the citizens of Trabue Woods in the April 15, 1919 newspaper article?

4. Why did the citizens of Trabue Woods raise the money for the colored school when the County would not?

5. How long did the "Jim Crow" era last? How did it come to an end?

LIVING HISTORY ASSIGNMENT

1. Interview Mr. John Allen, the elder who organized the NAACP during the 1960's and was a civil rights activist. If you do not live in Charlotte County, you can interview an elder who was involved in the civil rights movement in your community. Write a report about the civil rights movement in Charlotte County.

2. Watch the video series, "Eyes on the Prize". Talk to an elder and write a report about the civil rights movement in Charlotte County or the community in which you live.

THINK ABOUT IT

1. What did "success" mean to the African American
    pioneers who settled in Punta Gorda?

2. How did the values of the pioneers help them to have
    successful lives and to establish a successful community
    despite hardships?

3. How can the values of the African American pioneers
    who establish Trabue Woods help you to have a
    successful life?

THANK YOU

My sincere thank you to those who helped to make this book possible. First of all thank you to Yolanda Marion for all of your assistance, especially for taking and choosing photographs. Thank you to the Charlotte Sun and especially to Janine Smith for the willingness to let me read the very "delicate" old copies of the Punta Gorda Herald. Thank you to Bill MacDonald for his assistance in finding microfiche of old editions of the Punta Gorda Herald, and special thanks to Richard Carey for assistance with graphic work.

Aoishima Research Institute presents

The Character Education and Cultural Preservation Book Development Project

- We offer a curriculum development program that enables entities to develop character/values education and cultural preservation programs.
- We assist clients from Consultation through the Publishing of the materials.
- At the end of the process clients will have published texts that can be used for their character/values education and cultural preservation needs.

The following is an excerpt explaining to children the importance of values. This excerpt is from the book, *The Trabue Woods Book on Values*:

"WHY WE SHOULD LEARN ABOUT VALUES"

Values are what a group of people feel are important. Our values help us to decide what is right or wrong. They guide our actions. They are like signs on the highway, they point out the right direction in which we are to go. Our values help to determine our character. When we say that a person has good character, we are talking about their values.

This book is about values. One way in which we can learn about values is to study history and learn about the values of historical figures. In this book, we will learn about the values of a group of African American pioneers who settled in southwest Florida in 1885, and helped to establish the town of Trabue, later called Punta Gorda, on the Charlotte Harbor. While these African Americans lived in many parts of what became known as Charlotte County, they established their own special community named Trabue Woods."

For more information please contact:
Martha R. Bireda, Ph.D.

The Bireda Group, P.O. Box 510818, Punta Gorda, Florida 33951
Telefax: (941) 639-2914
E-mail: biredagrp@aol.com or mail@aoishima-research.com

AOISHIMA RESEARCH INSTITUTE

CULTURAL PRESERVATION WORKSHOP SERIES

Traditional African American Values

1. **Olowali: The Child Returns Home**

   Focuses on how traditional values and cultural integrity can be restored in African American communities.

2. **Reclaiming The Cultural Self**

   Learning how to overcome attachment to cultural values other than one's own (cultural alienation) and to reconstruct belief and value systems that promote a culturally-affirmed life.

3. **Cultural Legacy: Values That Support and Sustain**

   (Presented at the Geraldine Wilson Seminar of the 36th Annual Conference of the National Black Child Development Institute)

   An examination of the values that helped African Americans (1885 - 1925) to survive and build thriving communities while living through one of the most difficult periods African Americans faced, with the exception of slavery. Focuses on the pioneers of the Trabue Woods community in Punta Gorda, Florida.

4. **Lessons From The Ancestors**

   Addresses how the beliefs and values of the ancestors can be applied to solve problems and live more fully in the 21st century.

5. **Community History That Every African American Child Should Know**

   Strategies to help African American youth learn the essentials of their local history.

6. **The Essentials of Developing A Cultural Repository**

   Strategies for helping community organizations collect, preserve, and educate regarding local history.

For more information please contact:

Martha R. Bireda, Ph.D.
The Bireda Group,
P.O. Box 510818
Punta Gorda, Florida 33951

Telefax: (941) 639-2914

E-mail: biredagrp@aol.com or mail@aoishima-research.com

For Teachers, Parents, Counselors, and the General Community

PATHWAY TO CHANGE:

A GUIDE TO PERSONAL TRANSFORMATION

This book provides a "path" or blueprint to free the reader from the societal limitations, personal myths, and erroneous beliefs that prevents the full experience and expression of one's personal power.

Pathway to Change –

- Addresses the four crucial issues that contribute to one's being "stuck" on patterns that are non-productive and self-destructive; a sense of victimization; a sense powerlessness, the experience of a crisis in values, and spiritual emptiness.
- Helps reader to overcome "being a victim".
- Helps the reader to understand "the dynamics of power".
- Offers an alternative to the value system based on consumerism and materialism.
- Provides a way for the reader to re-connect to a sense of purpose.
- Creates an awareness of the root causes of the feelings, choices, and behaviors that keep one disempowered.
- Provides a system for modifying negative and self-destructive beliefs and values.
- Includes exercises for helping one to develop skills in managing emotions, problem-solving, decision-making, and life planning.
- Provides strategies for applying the cognitive restructuring concepts discussed in the book to one's major life arenas, e.g. personal relationships, employment, etc.
- A reader-friendly way to understand how to change one's life from disempowerment to empowerment.

In the over 25 years of her professional career, Dr. Bireda has been committed to the empowered of individuals and groups. From co-dependency counselor to equity consultant, she has facilitated groups, developed curricula, and written about issues of empowerment.

Dr. Bireda's previous work and experience with socio-cultural issues enabled her to develop *Pathway to Change*, a program that been remarkable in its ability to transform the lives of the individuals who have used it.